Saint Francis of Assisi Speaks 1

Published by Abba Books LLC
abbabooksllc@gmail.com
Copyright © 2023 Marie-Josée Thibault

All Rights Reserved

No part of this publication may be reproduced, distributed, or transmitted in any form or by any means, including photocopying, recording, or other electronic or mechanical methods, without the prior written permission of the publisher.

First Edition, 2023
Designed and Edited by Abba Books LLC
ISBN: 979-8-9897259-3-9

Abba Books LLC
34972 Newark Blvd, #441
Newark, CA 94560

www.abbamyfatheriloveyou.com
https://www.facebook.com/AbbaILoveYouBooks/

Thy Peace on Earth must be achieved. No light, no litany must be spared to honor Thy Grace.
-Saint Paul

Contents

Preface VI	Chap 16 37	Chap 32 77
Chap 1 1	Chap 17 39	Chap 33 79
Chap 2 3	Chap 18 43	Chap 34 81
Chap 3 5	Chap 19 45	Chap 35 83
Chap 4 7	Chap 20 47	Chap 36 87
Chap 5 9	Chap 21 51	Chap 37 89
Chap 6 13	Chap 22 53	Chap 38 91
Chap 7 15	Chap 23 55	Chap 39 93
Chap 8 17	Chap 24 57	Chap 40 95
Chap 9 19	Chap 25 59	Chap 41 99
Chap 10 21	Chap 26 63	Chap 42 101
Chap 11 25	Chap 27 65	Chap 43 103
Chap 12 27	Chap 28 67	Chap 44 105
Chap 13 29	Chap 29 69	Chap 45 107
Chap 14 31	Chap 30 71	Chap 46 111
Chap 15 33	Chap 31 75	

Preface

Readers of this collection from Heaven, welcome to this wonderfully edifying series written by Saint Francis of Assisi! I implore you to read these books on a daily basis as part of your devotional practice. This guide to Christian living is rich, unique, and perfectly adapted to modern life, spurred by the fact that Francis visits us regularly. He is aware of the exact sorrows and controversies that affect contemporary society. His instructions and training will be miraculously useful to you in your everyday life.

Francis is very gentle and humble when he visits me. His prayers are beautiful and transformative, and they arouse pain in the center of my left hand (unlike Padre Pio, whose visits arouse pain in the center of my right hand).

Live out all the lessons given in these blessed books and benefit from the consecration and extraordinary assistance of Saint Francis of Assisi!

Francis, I love you!

Marie-Josée

Saint Francis of Assisi Speaks

My friends, my brothers and sisters, all the children of God the Father Almighty, listen to me well. This Message is of utmost importance in that it concerns your future on earth. I speak with you from Heaven, where I dwell since my passage that is death in 1226. Heaven, of which I dreamed during my journey on earth, that is to say, the Heavenly Kingdom of God, is more majestic, more sublime, and more extraordinary than you could ever imagine. Paradise that has been promised, my friends, my brothers and sisters, I promise you too, in the Name of the Father, and of the Son, and of the Holy Spirit, through this wonderful book blessed by God. I say unto you, I say unto you verily, I am Saint Francis of Assisi and I speak with you today from Paradise where I dwell. Glory be to the Father, and to the Son, and to the Holy Spirit, as it was in the beginning, is now and ever shall be, world without end! Amen. Alleluia!

Saint Francis of Assisi Speaks

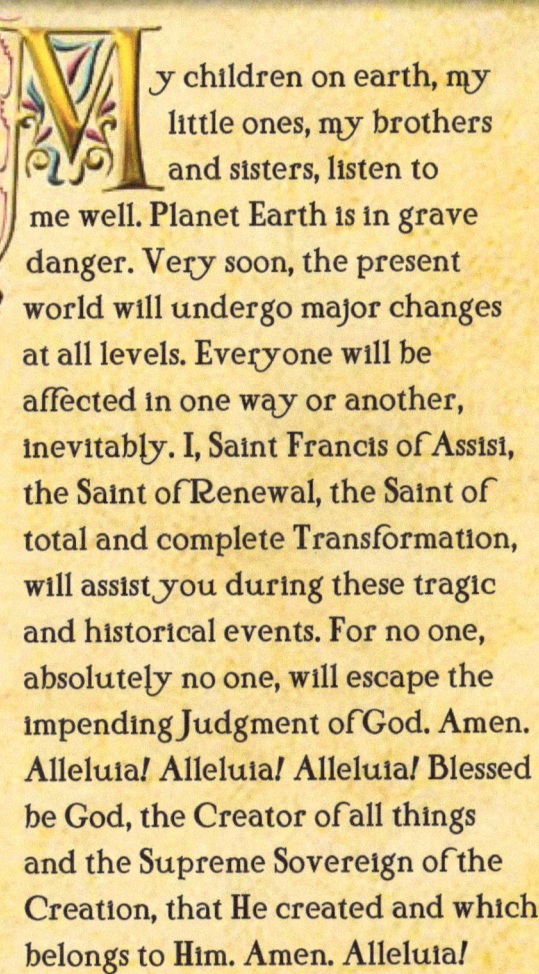

My children on earth, my little ones, my brothers and sisters, listen to me well. Planet Earth is in grave danger. Very soon, the present world will undergo major changes at all levels. Everyone will be affected in one way or another, inevitably. I, Saint Francis of Assisi, the Saint of Renewal, the Saint of total and complete Transformation, will assist you during these tragic and historical events. For no one, absolutely no one, will escape the impending Judgment of God. Amen. Alleluia! Alleluia! Alleluia! Blessed be God, the Creator of all things and the Supreme Sovereign of the Creation, that He created and which belongs to Him. Amen. Alleluia!

Saint Francis of Assisi Speaks

My friends, my brothers and sisters, listen to me well. The Mysteries of life on earth will be very much clearer for you in the very near future. The book you are holding in your hands contains Mystical Revelations important for the health of your soul, and especially for the transformation of your heart. For your Fundamental Transformation, that is to say, the Christification of your soul that resides in your heart, is part of the mission that God the Father Almighty assigned me regarding you, dear child. For God is Merciful unto you, here and now, through this book blessed by Him that you are holding in your hands, fruit of the Merits and the Love of Saint Paul the Apostle. Alleluia! Alleluia! Alleluia! Blessed be God the Father Almighty, God of Life, God of Charity, God of Truth, and God of Love! Amen. Alleluia!

Saint Francis of Assisi Speaks

My friends, my brothers and sisters, listen to me well. Earth is in danger! Yes, my friends, the whole world will suffer catastrophic changes unprecedented in its history. My role is to prepare you, to teach you, to support you, and to protect you during these events that are fast approaching. The book you are holding in your hands, dear friends, dear souls, will be a precious help to you in order to survive the tribulations that are fast approaching. Read this book, read it again, study it, share it — for God the Father Almighty has made it a gift to you personally. Alleluia! Alleluia! Alleluia! Blessed be God the Father Almighty, God of Benevolence and God of Charity! Amen. Alleluia!

Saint Francis of Assisi Speaks

My friends, my brothers and sisters, listen to me well. The Words that I speak unto you are Sacred, for the vessel used by God for the transmission of these Words is the essence of Saint Paul, Marie-Josée T. Marie-Josée has been trained for this mission well before her birth, according to the Will of God. The scope of her life on earth is a private matter between God the Father and herself, through Jesus Christ our Savior and the Immaculate Heart of Mary. Her life on earth is infinitely protected and guided by God the Father Almighty Himself. Beware, those who oppose the mission of a vessel on earth made Sacred by God, for God Himself is the One Whom you oppose. Alleluia! Alleluia! Alleluia! Blessed be Marie-Josée, the essence of Saint Paul on earth, who accomplishes her mission to perfection. Amen. Alleluia!

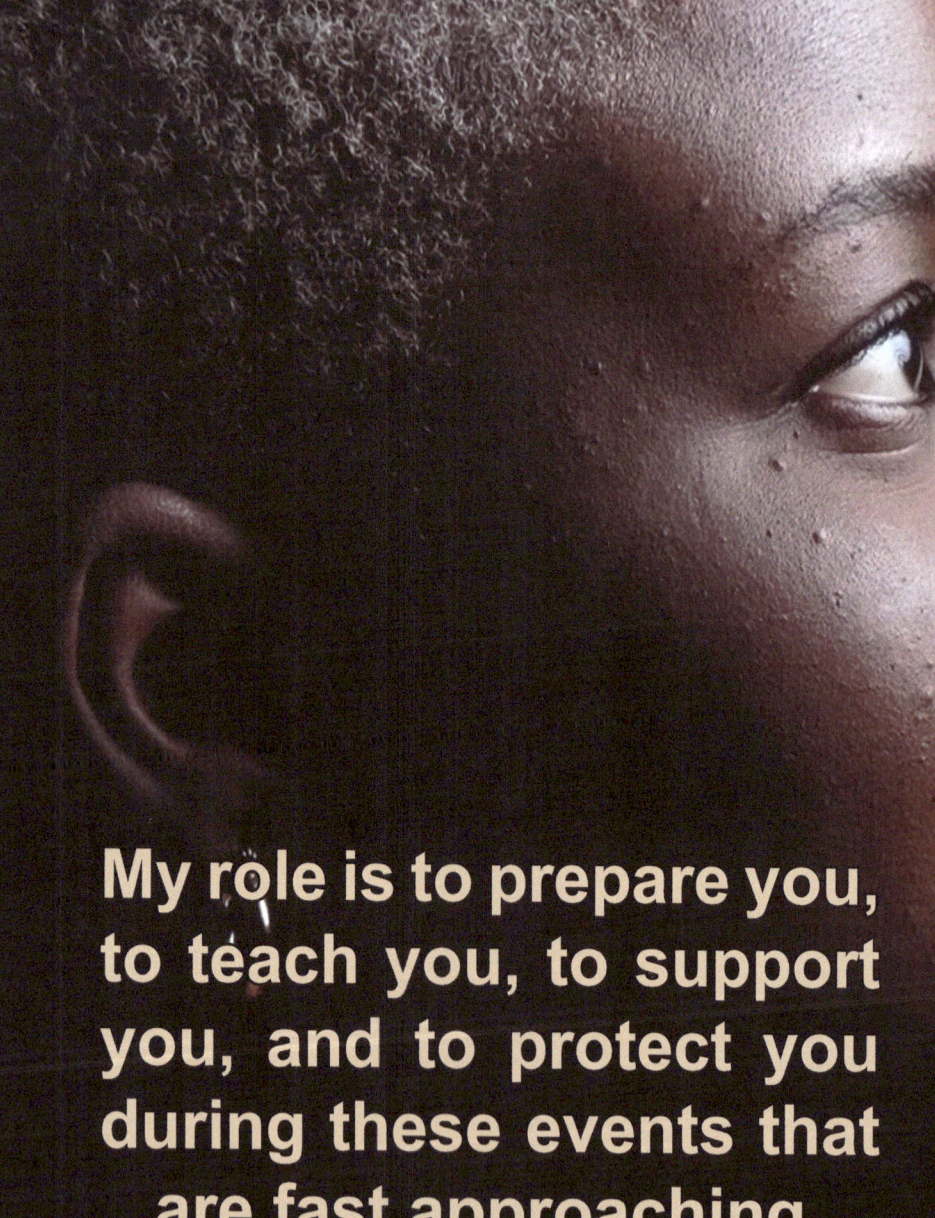

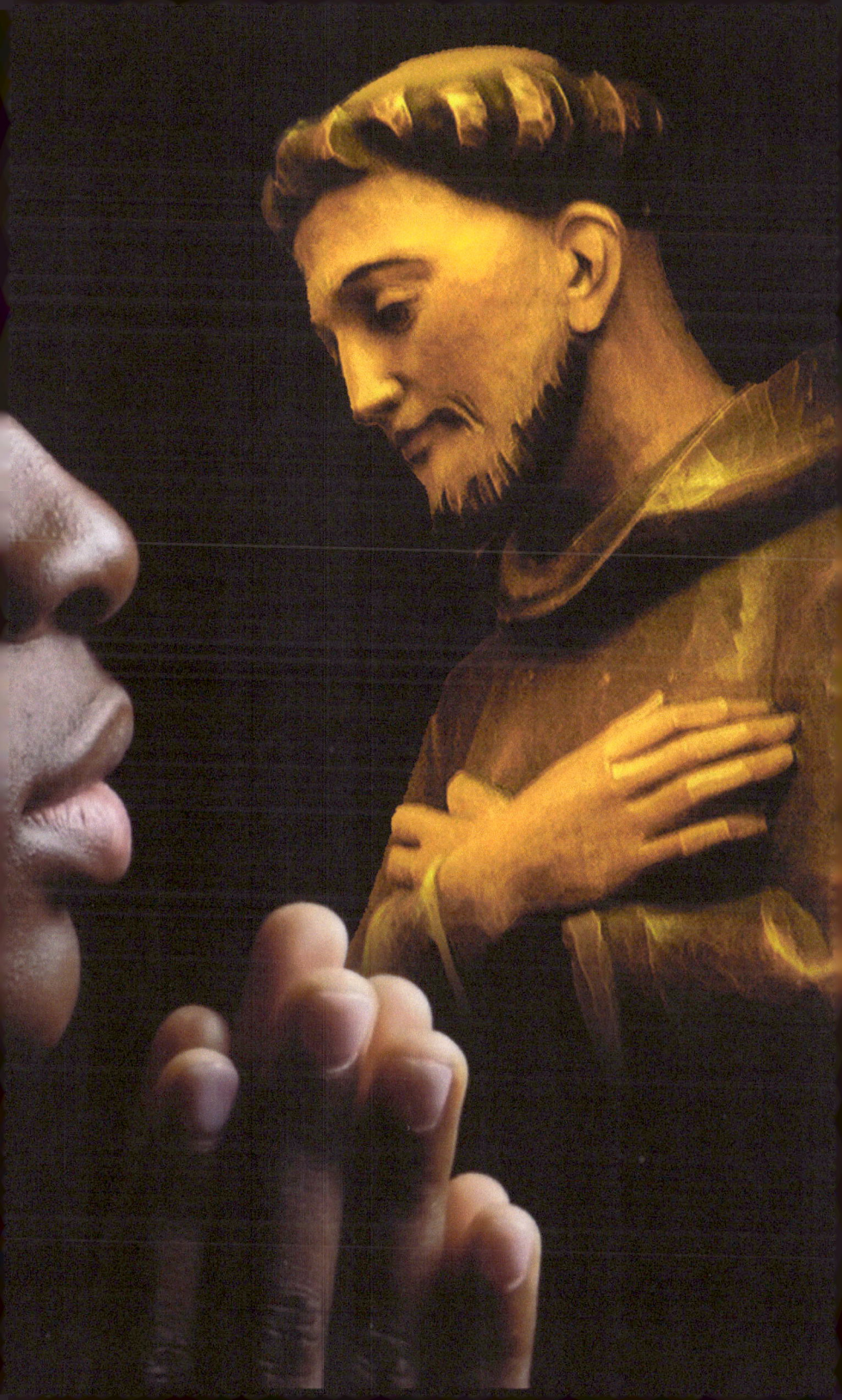

Saint Francis of Assisi Speaks

My friends, my brothers and sisters, listen to me well. The tragic end of this civilization which is at your door is not a coincidence. Of course not! This unfortunate and disastrous outcome is the result of an enormous worldwide debt — in fact, incalculable — toward God. Such scandal! Such nonsense! Such cruelty! Such infamy! So much abuse and neglect! The global debt of the whole earth toward God can only be paid with events of the same magnitude, in order to restore the balance between the inferior Energies and the Superior Energies of the universe. My role here, through this book blessed by God, and using the Sacred vessel that is Marie-Josée T., is to instruct you and to transform you in order to survive the events approaching; in fact, for you, dear little soul in my hands, the events that will follow will be a source of liberation. Alleluia! Alleluia! Alleluia! Blessed is he who hears my Sacred Words today, the Sacred Words of Saint Francis of Assisi, for this one shall be saved. Amen. Alleluia!

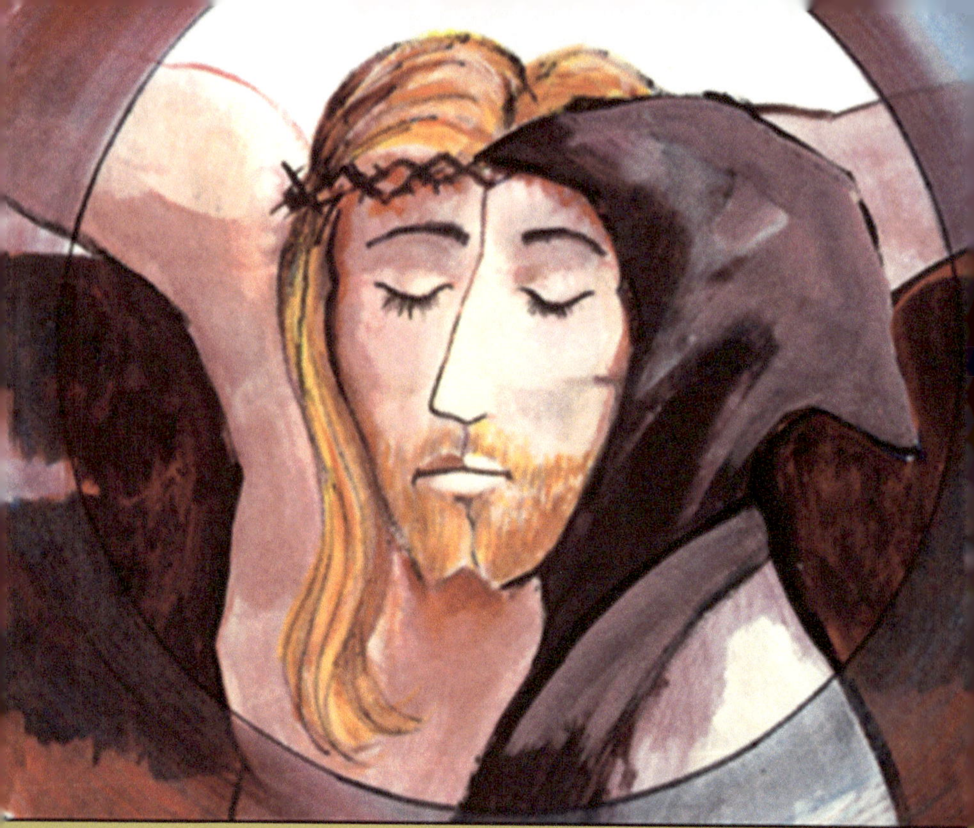

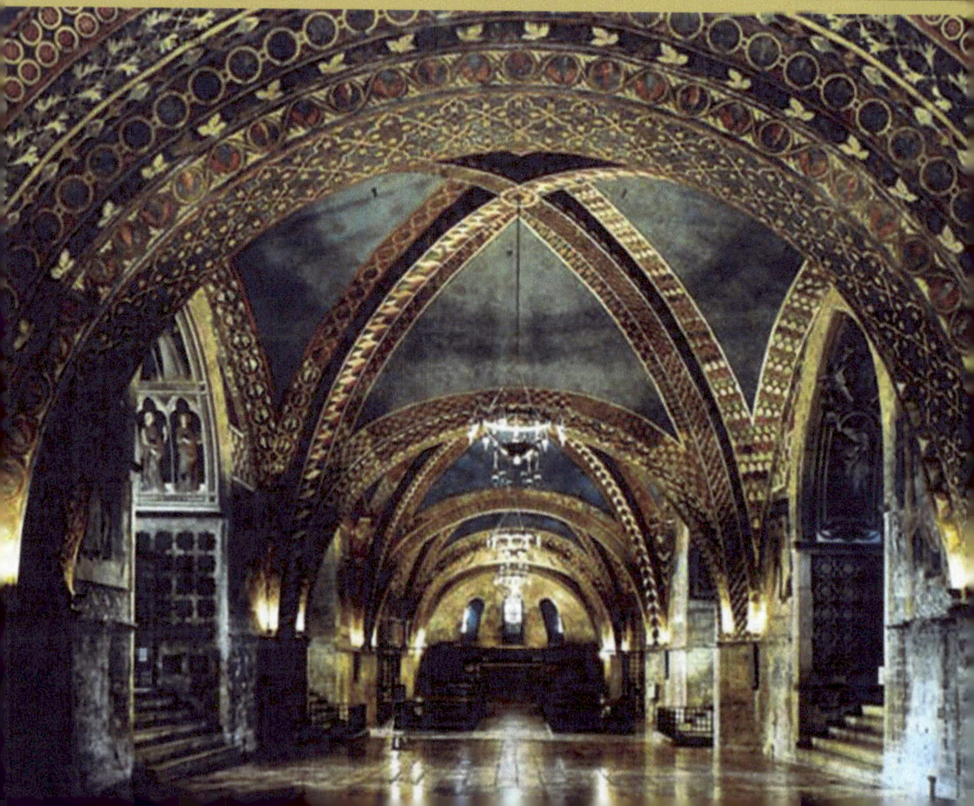

Saint Francis of Assisi Speaks

My friends, my brothers and sisters, listen to me well. Today marks a very critical period of your life. Not only are you introduced to Superior and Divine Teachings, but also and more importantly, your soul will begin once and for all the return journey toward the Father, and toward His Kingdom. For the ultimate goal of every soul on earth is its salvation, that is to say, its peaceful and joyful return to God, after the exile that is the life time on earth. Blessed are the souls who will be saved through the intercession of Saint Francis of Assisi! Convert today to Christ Jesus! Give yourself completely and eternally to God your Creator and your soul will be saved! Amen. Alleluia!

Saint Francis of Assisi Speaks

My friends, my brothers and sisters, listen to me well. The life you live on earth, although it seems very real and very tangible in the three dimensions that hold the support of your life, in fact, no longer exists. Whereof I am speaking with you, here in Paradise, events that are fast approaching, are, in fact, already accomplished. I wish to explain to you, dear soul, that here in Paradise, where time does not exist, represents in fact the future with regard to the temporal dimension where you live. However, here in Paradise where I dwell, planet Earth and all its history, is part of the past. Do you see? That is why we know the upcoming events, for we have seen them, and we know the seriousness and horror of the world drama that is being prepared. We know its duration and we know its outcome. That is why we strive to inform you, to strengthen you, and to prepare you for the inevitable events. Do you see? This tragic wave will pass, and thereafter will rise on earth a New Day, the Era of the New Sun, based solely on Christ — and that is to say, the Return of Christ in all His Glory and in all His Majesty. Yes, the Era of the New Sun, we have seen it! Oh yes, we have seen it! Amen. Alleluia!

Saint Francis of Assisi Speaks

My friends, my brothers and sisters, listen to me well. The suffering experienced by Christ on the Cross — suffering that was the utmost extraordinarily painful that no man has ever experienced — has earned you access to Paradise, to the extent that you accept to live also the Way of the Cross as He lived. Living one's life according to the Teaching of Christ, according to the Pain of Christ, according to the Charity of Christ, according to the Love and Forgiveness of Christ, will merit you to obtain the Promise of God's Kingdom. For Christ is really the Way, the Truth, and the Life. I say unto you, I say unto you verily, all that is not of Christ will be obliterated and all that is of Christ will live forever. Amen. Alleluia!

Saint Francis of Assisi Speaks

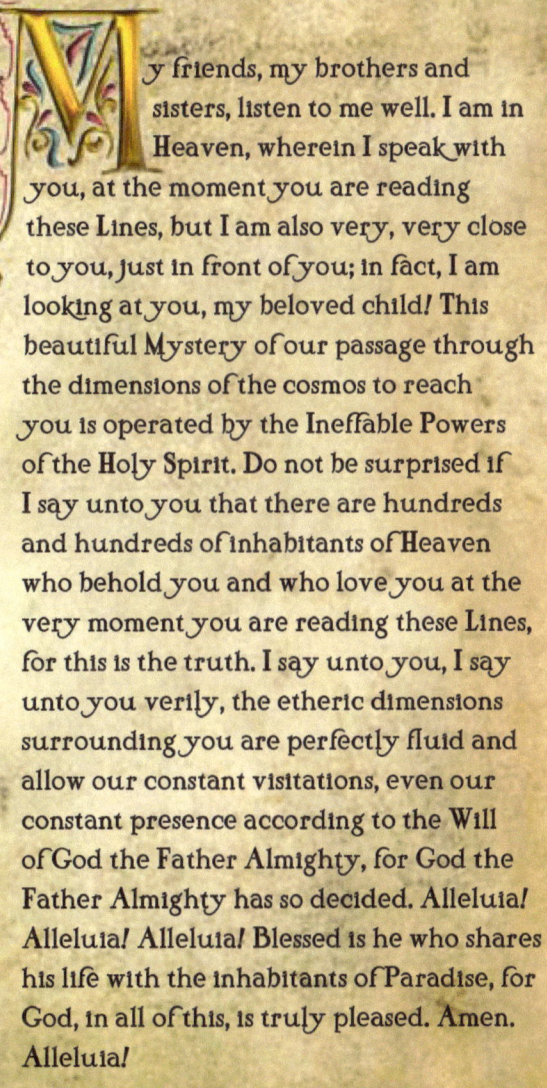

My friends, my brothers and sisters, listen to me well. I am in Heaven, wherein I speak with you, at the moment you are reading these Lines, but I am also very, very close to you, just in front of you; in fact, I am looking at you, my beloved child! This beautiful Mystery of our passage through the dimensions of the cosmos to reach you is operated by the Ineffable Powers of the Holy Spirit. Do not be surprised if I say unto you that there are hundreds and hundreds of inhabitants of Heaven who behold you and who love you at the very moment you are reading these Lines, for this is the truth. I say unto you, I say unto you verily, the etheric dimensions surrounding you are perfectly fluid and allow our constant visitations, even our constant presence according to the Will of God the Father Almighty, for God the Father Almighty has so decided. Alleluia! Alleluia! Alleluia! Blessed is he who shares his life with the inhabitants of Paradise, for God, in all of this, is truly pleased. Amen. Alleluia!

Saint Francis of Assisi
(1182-1226)

Saint Francis of Assisi Speaks

My friends, my brothers and sisters, listen to me well. The events that are fast approaching will be sources of extreme emotion among all the inhabitants of the earth. Non-believers will invest their hopes of survival in the government and the military forces that will disappoint them. Believers, on the contrary, will invest their hopes of survival in God and His Army of Heaven to deliver them from the spirit of Satan. I say unto you, I say unto you verily, only believers in God converted to Christ Jesus and dedicated to the Virgin Mary will be saved, body and soul. Alleluia! Alleluia! Alleluia! Blessed are those who believe, for faith is the only salvation of humanity. Amen. Alleluia!

Saint Francis of Assisi Speaks

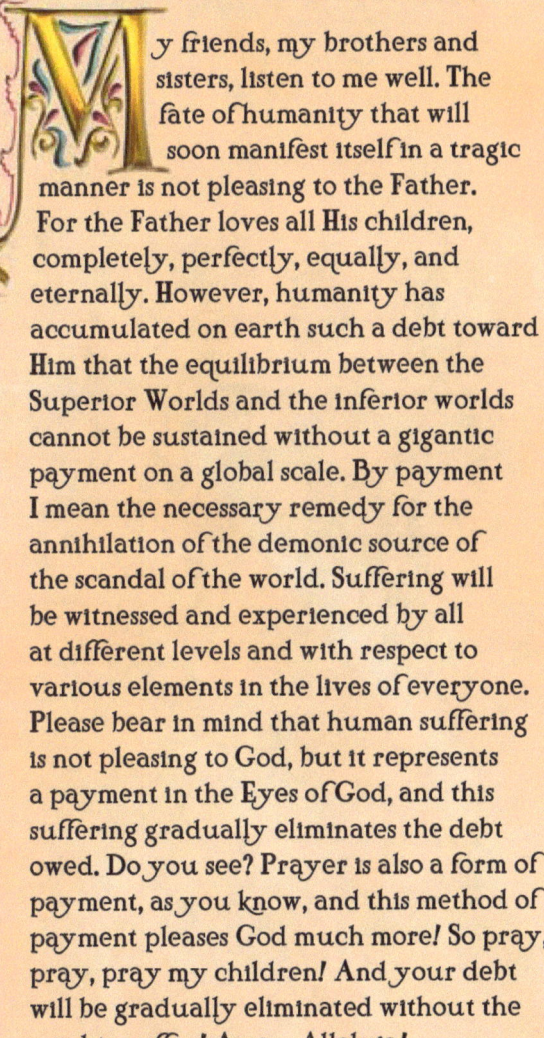

My friends, my brothers and sisters, listen to me well. The fate of humanity that will soon manifest itself in a tragic manner is not pleasing to the Father. For the Father loves all His children, completely, perfectly, equally, and eternally. However, humanity has accumulated on earth such a debt toward Him that the equilibrium between the Superior Worlds and the inferior worlds cannot be sustained without a gigantic payment on a global scale. By payment I mean the necessary remedy for the annihilation of the demonic source of the scandal of the world. Suffering will be witnessed and experienced by all at different levels and with respect to various elements in the lives of everyone. Please bear in mind that human suffering is not pleasing to God, but it represents a payment in the Eyes of God, and this suffering gradually eliminates the debt owed. Do you see? Prayer is also a form of payment, as you know, and this method of payment pleases God much more! So pray, pray, pray my children! And your debt will be gradually eliminated without the need to suffer! Amen. Alleluia!

Saint Francis of Assisi Speaks

My friends, my brothers and sisters, I love you; listen to me well. The fate of your body made of dust on earth is already determined by God the Father Almighty. It is certain death of the physical body, in a manner chosen by Him alone, and at the time chosen by Him alone. The fate of your soul (and of your Spirit) is evolving, depending on your spiritual progress and your level of conversion to Christ Jesus, His Beloved Son, our Savior to all. Do not delay giving yourself completely to Him, to Christ the Savior, One in the Holy Trinity. Today, pray, pray, pray, gather in churches around the world to express unequivocally your dedication to Him, the Shepherd Christ, our King and our Master! Amen. Alleluia!

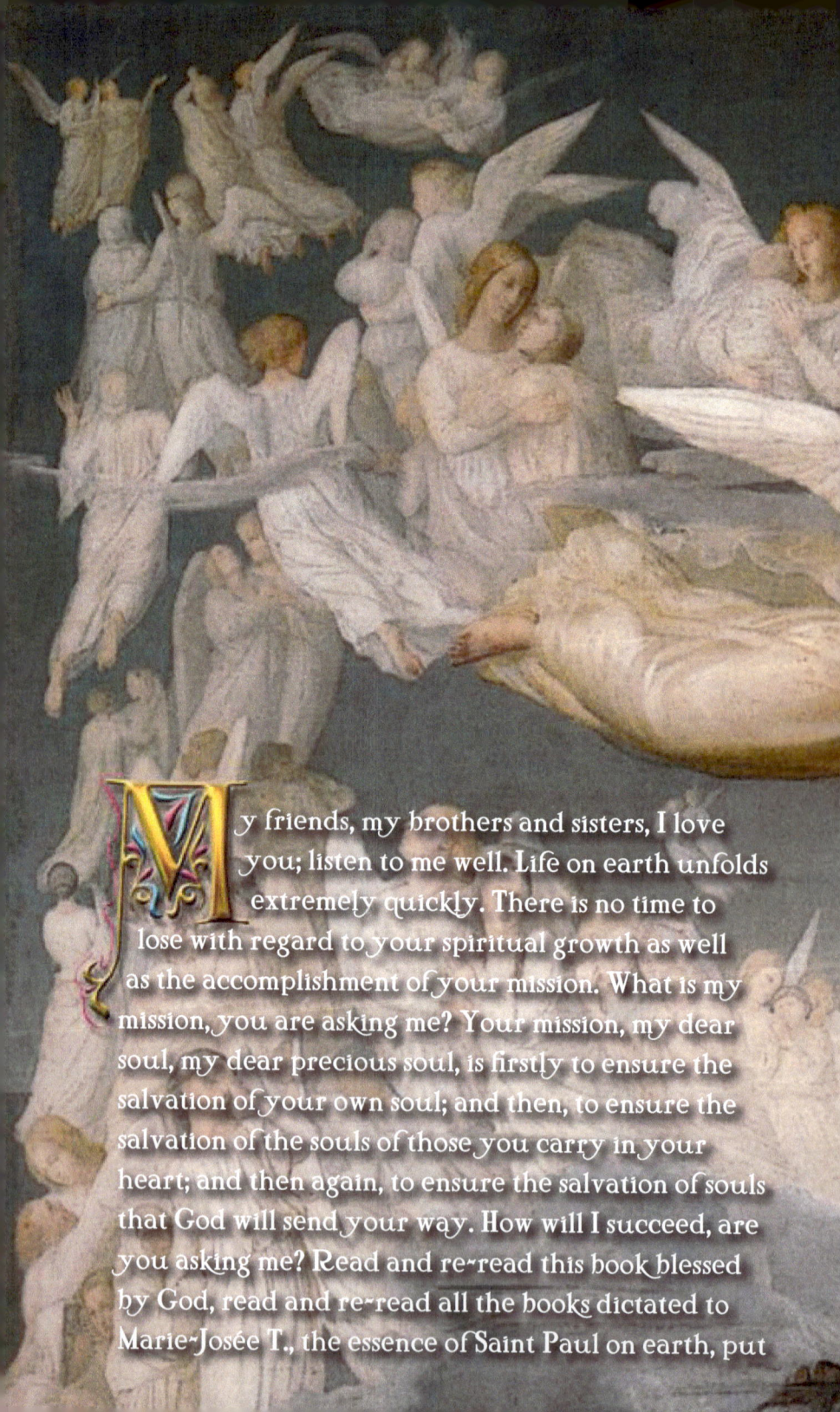

My friends, my brothers and sisters, I love you; listen to me well. Life on earth unfolds extremely quickly. There is no time to lose with regard to your spiritual growth as well as the accomplishment of your mission. What is my mission, you are asking me? Your mission, my dear soul, my dear precious soul, is firstly to ensure the salvation of your own soul; and then, to ensure the salvation of the souls of those you carry in your heart; and then again, to ensure the salvation of souls that God will send your way. How will I succeed, are you asking me? Read and re-read this book blessed by God, read and re-read all the books dictated to Marie-Josée T., the essence of Saint Paul on earth, put

Saint Francis of Assisi Speaks

into practice the instructions given, and let us have the pleasure and boundless joy to assist you and to accomplish God's Great Plan of salvation through you. For your beautiful little soul was chosen by God the Father Almighty Himself through Jesus, Christ Jesus, our Lord and our God, the Most Blessed Virgin Mary, and by myself as well as by all the inhabitants of Paradise who know you very well and who love you, in order to bear much fruit on earth. Thus, you will become for Him, for Christ the Savior, a true disciple. Alleluia! Alleluia! Alleluia! Blessed is the soul chosen to become a disciple of Jesus, for this soul deserves Paradise. Amen. Alleluia!

Saint Francis of Assisi Speaks

15

My children, my brothers and sisters, listen to me well. Here and now, most dear soul, very precious soul, I desire to see a giant step accomplished during your journey toward God. I wish to see this day — just as God the Father Almighty Who is watching you and Who loves you — a decisive gesture, an openness of heart, a strong emotion impassioned for Jesus Christ our Savior. Say your prayers from the depth of your heart (the deepest of your entire life), express your love and forgiveness to those around you in a way clearer and more determined than before, be kind and charitable to all who come near you, including all the creatures of God. Today, my beloved child, God the Father Almighty leans toward you much more closely than you could imagine, in order to give you His Divine Mercy. Express all your gratitude today by behaving like His loving child, just and courageous! Amen. Alleluia!

MUST BE ACHIEVED

Saint Francis of Assisi Speaks

16

My friends, my brothers and sisters, I love you; listen to me well. Here in Paradise, everything is implemented in order to accelerate your spiritual growth and ensure your royal entrance among us after the passage that is death. Your soul, so precious to all the inhabitants of Paradise — and especially to the Father — is flooded with Christic Light at any time of the day and night, well beyond your perception of this Miracle of Divine Providence. For your soul, my dear child, is now in our hands — the hands of the Father, the Holy Spirit, the Virgin Mary, Christ Jesus, Saint Paul the Apostle, all the Saints in Paradise, the Angels of God, and the pure Souls — through this book blessed by God and for the rest of your life and for Eternity. Alleluia! Alleluia! Alleluia! Blessed be this book filled with Treasures and Wonders of Paradise! Amen. Alleluia!

Saint Francis of Assisi Speaks

My friends, my brothers and sisters, I love you; listen to me well. Life on earth, despite its contradictions and vicissitudes, is a path of the awakening of consciousness. The Being deposits its essence in a body, in a family, in a particular city, and puts everything in place in order to raise its essence to its Spiritual Reality. The Being, as explained by Saint Paul in his book I am Saint Paul the Apostle, is your inner Light, the Light derived from the Father Almighty, the Solar Father. The Being is your intimate Father, your Source of Life, your beginning and your end. When you die, your soul returns to your intimate Father, and the intimate Father returns to the Father Almighty. Do you see? It is fundamental in your life to awaken yourself completely to your Spiritual Reality. The Absolute Guide in order to proceed to the awakening of consciousness and the return of your essence toward your intimate Father, and then toward the Father Almighty, is Christ, our Savior. Alleluia! Alleluia! Alleluia! Blessed be Christ, our Master on the path of the awakening of consciousness! Amen. Alleluia!

His Mission is clear: Christ is the Way, the Truth, and the Life of the Spirit who becomes realized Spiritually and completely in the Plenitude of the intimate Father and the Solar Father.

Saint Francis of Assisi Speaks

My friends, my brothers and sisters, listen to me. Today, more than any other day of your life so far, Heaven has opened for you! Look well around you, my friends, my children, and be assured of my Heavenly Presence, as well as the Presence of several other inhabitants of Paradise. For today, through this wonderful book where the Treasures from Heaven are buried, fruit of the Divine Mercy won by the merits of the work of the Five Crosses, I am there nearby you, I, Saint Francis of Assisi, the Saint of Total Transformation, the Saint of Renewal, the father of the Franciscans, whose Holy souls have rejoiced our Lord and God, the humble father of the Friars Minor, and I love you. I am Saint Francis and I love you! Amen. Alleluia!

Saint Francis of Assisi Speaks

My children, my brothers and sisters, I love you so much, listen to me well. Today, through this book blessed by God, the Angels in Heaven and the Saints in Paradise (including myself) offer you a Heavenly and Glorious embrace in the joy and gladness of welcoming you here in Paradise, after the passage that is death. This life will soon be complete, dear heart, and nothing can prolong your life on earth if this is the Father's Will in this regard. On the contrary, the life of the soul — I mean here its salvation and the royal entrance to Paradise awaiting you — is promised to you today, thanks to the Divine Mercy offered here. Alleluia! Alleluia! Alleluia! Blessed be the book you are holding in your hands, Miracle of Life and Miracle of Peace to the soul seeking God! Amen. Alleluia!

Saint Francis of Assisi Speaks

My friends, my brothers and sisters, I love you so much, listen to me well. Today, more than any other day in your life, be happy! Whatever the events of the day or night, the ecological disasters you observe on earth, the aberrant contradictions of modern society, the turbulence in your personal life, the demands and the fatigue generated by work, the economic difficulties, today, my beloved child, be happy! Be happy for true and good reasons! Be happy, for I speak with you, dear little soul in my humble Miraculous hands, I, Saint Francis of Assisi; be happy for Christ our Lord and God has saved you; be happy for God the Father Almighty has granted you Mercy this day blessed by Him; be happy for the Kingdom of God, in all its splendor that you can not imagine, is awaiting you...Be happy! Amen. Alleluia!

Today, through this book blessed by God, the Angels in Heaven, the Saints in Paradise (including myself), offer you a Heavenly and Glorious embrace in the joy and gladness of welcoming you here in Paradise, after the passage that is death.

~ Saint Francis

My children, my brothers and sisters, my friends in the Good News of Christ the Savior, I love you; listen to me well. Today, through your prayers and your inner recollection, I wish to see you in a state of true contrition of your sins. All the mistakes committed in your life toward God and toward human beings, including neglect, abuse, manipulation, lies, etc., must be deposited at the Feet of the Cross of Christ the Savior. Simply say: "My Lord Jesus Christ, my Savior and my God, I deposit at your Sacred Feet the sum of all the sins of my life. My heart cries at the sight of so many offenses committed against the Holy Trinity and my fellow human being. Have pity on me, my Lord, my Jesus, my Christ, my Savior, my God, and pour forth unto me Your Infinite Divine Mercy if it be Your Will, and the Father's Will, God the Father Almighty. By the operations of the Holy Spirit, God the Holy Spirit, Spirit of God the Father and Spirit of God the Son, proceed today to the purification of my soul and of my Spirit. I pray through the Holy and Sacred Name of Jesus and the Immaculate Heart of Mary. Saint Francis of Assisi, intercede for me. Amen." Alleluia!

Saint Francis of Assisi Speaks

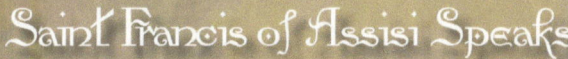

My children, my brothers and sisters, my friends in the Good News, I love you; listen to me well. Here in Paradise, today, everything is implemented in order to accelerate your royal entrance among us. The Angels of God, the Saints in Paradise, the pure Souls, redoubled their efforts and prayers in order to give you all the solutions and all the remedies necessary for your spiritual growth. For your soul must be purified, dear child, in the Eyes of God and in the Eyes of God solely. We know what pleases God (and we know very well what displeases Him), so we can properly assist you regarding the preparation of your soul for the passage that is death. For God — Yes, God solely — will be the Judge of your soul. Amen. Alleluia! Blessed be your soul, all beautiful and all pure, white as snow in the Eyes of God! Amen. Alleluia!

Saint Francis of Assisi Speaks

My children, my brothers and sisters, my friends in the Good News, I love you so much, listen to me well. Today, my heart, dear precious soul in my hands, be and remain in a renewed and transformed state. Look around you with renewed eyes, a purified heart, an exalted soul, a body transformed by the Christic Light that I am pouring forth unto you at this moment I am speaking with you. For today, dear friend, dear reader, the Christ, our Savior and our God, has grown within your heart. Yes, my child, Christ, who was already living within your heart, is now occupying a much larger space, more than you can imagine. For today, my heart and my joy, the Lord will speak with you. Listen carefully to His Divine Teaching. Verily, verily I say unto you, Christ Jesus, our Lord and our God, will speak with you. Amen. Alleluia!

Saint Francis of Assisi Speaks

My children, my brothers and sisters, my friends in the Good News, I love you so much, listen to me well. Here, now, at this very moment you are reading these Lines, say this out loud: "My Lord, my God, my Jesus Christ, forgive me my sins and purify my soul. I pray to you today with a fervor more intense, with a deeper faith, with a heart more sincere, than yesterday. My Jesus, my Christ, my Lord and my God, I love you! Oh yes, how much I love you! Amen." Alleluia!

Saint Francis of Assisi Speaks

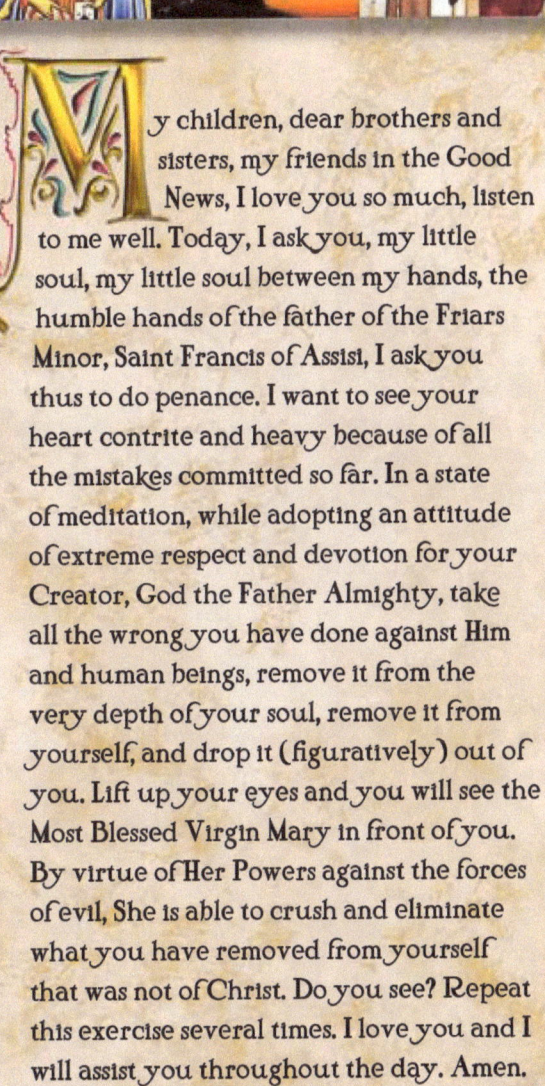

My children, dear brothers and sisters, my friends in the Good News, I love you so much, listen to me well. Today, I ask you, my little soul, my little soul between my hands, the humble hands of the father of the Friars Minor, Saint Francis of Assisi, I ask you thus to do penance. I want to see your heart contrite and heavy because of all the mistakes committed so far. In a state of meditation, while adopting an attitude of extreme respect and devotion for your Creator, God the Father Almighty, take all the wrong you have done against Him and human beings, remove it from the very depth of your soul, remove it from yourself, and drop it (figuratively) out of you. Lift up your eyes and you will see the Most Blessed Virgin Mary in front of you. By virtue of Her Powers against the forces of evil, She is able to crush and eliminate what you have removed from yourself that was not of Christ. Do you see? Repeat this exercise several times. I love you and I will assist you throughout the day. Amen. Alleluia!

Pray, do penance, lift up your eyes and you will see the Most Blessed Virgin Mary in front of you

~ Saint Francis

Saint Francis of Assisi Speaks

My children, my brothers and sisters, my friends in the Good News, listen to me well. Today, my dear hearts, all gathered in my Divine embrace, let us pray to God: "God our Father Almighty, You Who are the Creator of all things visible and invisible, I pray to you, I implore you, I ask you, from the very depth of my heart, for the Peace of Christ in the world, for the Glorious Return of Christ in the world, for a peaceful and smooth transition toward a new civilization based solely on Christ, our Savior and our God. I want to see this new civilization, my Father, I want to prepare its edification, I want to share in its glorious success, and I want to be a Child of the New Sun. I love you, my Father, my Creator, be Merciful to me and to the whole world. Amen." Alleluia! Dear heart, I want you to repeat this prayer several times this day. I love you. I am Saint Francis of Assisi and I love you. Amen. Alleluia!

Saint Francis of Assisi Speaks

My friends, my brothers and sisters, my children that I love so much, listen to me well. It is impossible for me to express all the joy I feel for being able to speak with you. I, Saint Francis of Assisi, the humble father of the Friars Minor, your Divine Friend in the Good News, your Holy intercessor before God the Father Almighty, embrace you with all the Love in Paradise. Such exaltation here in Paradise when a soul is in contact with us through this book blessed by God! For God is Merciful unto you, dear soul, through each Line you are reading contained in this collection, fruit of the merits earned by the work of the Five Crosses. Alleluia! Alleluia! Alleluia! Blessed is the Soul of Saint Paul the Apostle, for the work of the Five Crosses is realized through your soul, dear reader, to the delight of God. Amen. Alleluia!

Saint Francis of Assisi Speaks

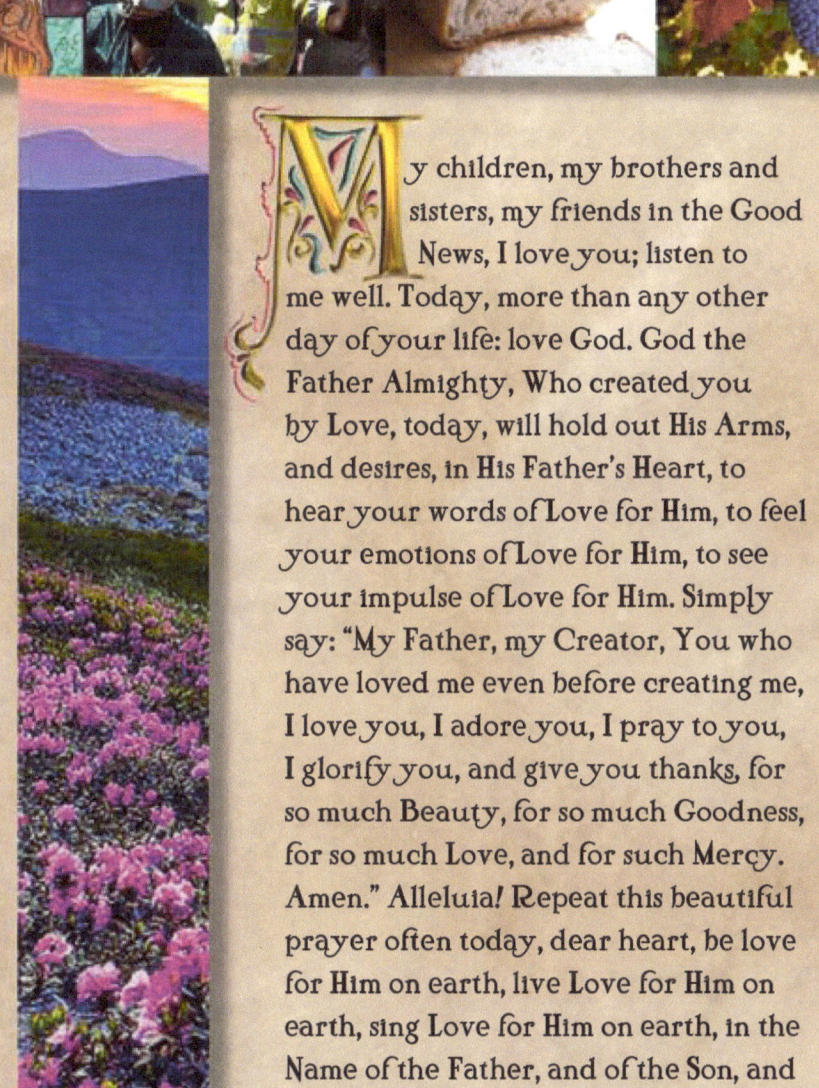

My children, my brothers and sisters, my friends in the Good News, I love you; listen to me well. Today, more than any other day of your life: love God. God the Father Almighty, Who created you by Love, today, will hold out His Arms, and desires, in His Father's Heart, to hear your words of Love for Him, to feel your emotions of Love for Him, to see your impulse of Love for Him. Simply say: "My Father, my Creator, You who have loved me even before creating me, I love you, I adore you, I pray to you, I glorify you, and give you thanks, for so much Beauty, for so much Goodness, for so much Love, and for such Mercy. Amen." Alleluia! Repeat this beautiful prayer often today, dear heart, be love for Him on earth, live Love for Him on earth, sing Love for Him on earth, in the Name of the Father, and of the Son, and of the Holy Spirit. Amen. Alleluia!

Saint Francis of Assisi Speaks

My children, my brothers and sisters, my friends in the Good News, I love you; listen to me well. Today, more than any other day of your life, love your Mother. Your Divine Mother, the Most Blessed Virgin Mary, has carried you in Her bosom from the very beginning of the Creation of the Universe, at the Cradle of Genesis. The Most Blessed Virgin Mary is the Mother of Christ, and due to the fact that Christ lives and dwells in every human heart (regardless of the personal belief in Him of the same heart), consequently, She is also your Mother, and this, as mentioned earlier, well before your birth — for your soul is Eternal, and it was created at the very beginning of Genesis. Do you see? Today, my dear soul in my humble hands, pray your rosary with a devotion never experienced until now, with renewed fervor and intimacy with your Heavenly Mother, with the sincerity of a child running into the arms of his mother. For She is there, in your heart, and She is awaiting you. Amen. Alleluia! Good Heavenly Mother, how much I love you!

Saint Francis of Assisi Speaks

My children, my brothers and sisters, my friends in the Good News, I love you; listen to me well. Today, although you may have done this in the past, bow down before a Cross. Take a crucifix (ideally with the Body of Christ on the Cross) and place it in your meditation room or in your bedroom. Then lie on your stomach before it, arms outstretched, and in a state of deep devotion and great respect, say the following prayer: "My Lord Jesus Christ, my Savior and my God, I love you, I adore you, I pray to you, forgive me my sins, for I am a poor sinner and evil has taken over me. Purify me, my sweet Jesus, deliver me from evil and all the obstacles that prevent me from seeing you, hearing you, and feeling you. Saint Francis of Assisi, intercede for me. Amen." Alleluia!

I, Saint Francis of Assisi, the humble father of the Friars Minor, your Divine Friend in the Good News, your Holy intercessor before God the Father Almighty, embrace you with all the Love in Paradise.

~ Saint Francis

My children, my brothers and sisters, my friends in the Good News, I love you; listen to me well. Today, my dear heart, I wish to see you happy and rejoicing, not because I am asking you, but rather because Christ gives you this profound and intimate inspiration. Do you see? Christ Jesus, present everywhere in the universe created by God, our Eternal Father to all, is in constant vibration in your heart, and this Presence at once Mystical and physical will intensify day by day according to the sincerity and the multitude of your prayers, of your devotions, and of our actions derived from Christ. Be Holy as Christ has taught you, as His Messengers have shown you, and shortly, very shortly, your desire to live every moment of your life with Him will be fullfilled. Amen. Alleluia!

Saint Francis of Assisi Speaks

Saint Francis of Assisi Speaks

My friends, my very dear children, my brothers and sisters, listen to me well. Today will be a different day for you. Today, my very dear heart, imagine a renewed world! Imagine a world without cruelty, without negligence, without abuse, without contradiction, without lies! Rest assured, very beautiful soul, that this world is already in place in the Superior Planes of the Creation, and will settle comfortably among you on earth. This new world, this New Sun, will be based solely on Christ, that is to say, on Love, Forgiveness, Charity, Unity, and Truth. This world, my very dear friends of the earth, will inevitably settle among you; and just as inevitably, the current world, which opposes Christ more and more, will be destroyed to make way for the New Sun. I say unto you, I say unto you verily, the end times are drawing near. Do not delay your prayers and preparations for the transition that is fast approaching. Continue to read this book blessed by God as well as all the books from this collection. The Divine Mercy you need is found therein. I love you. I am Saint Francis of Assisi and I love you! Amen. Alleluia!

Saint Francis of Assisi Speaks

My children, my brothers and sisters, my friends in the Good News, I love you so much. Today, dear friends, rejoice and be glad, for the Angels of God live among you. Yes, dear heart, your Guardian Angel stands even closer to you today, just behind and slightly to the right, and He ensures your protection and your spiritual growth for the rest of your life. Never forget: the Guardian Angels of those around you can also see you. In fact, the Guardian Angels of each of you communicate with each other, meet when two people come together, rejoice together at the spiritual progress of their protégés, support one another when progress is unfortunately too long or nonexistent, and work very hard in order to assist you at all levels of your life. For your Guardian Angel is the Light of the Father, the Light of Love, and the Light of Divine Protection. Be thankful to God the Almighty Father for the Benedictions brought about by the Guardian Angels everywhere on earth. Amen. Alleluia!

Saint Francis of Assisi Speaks

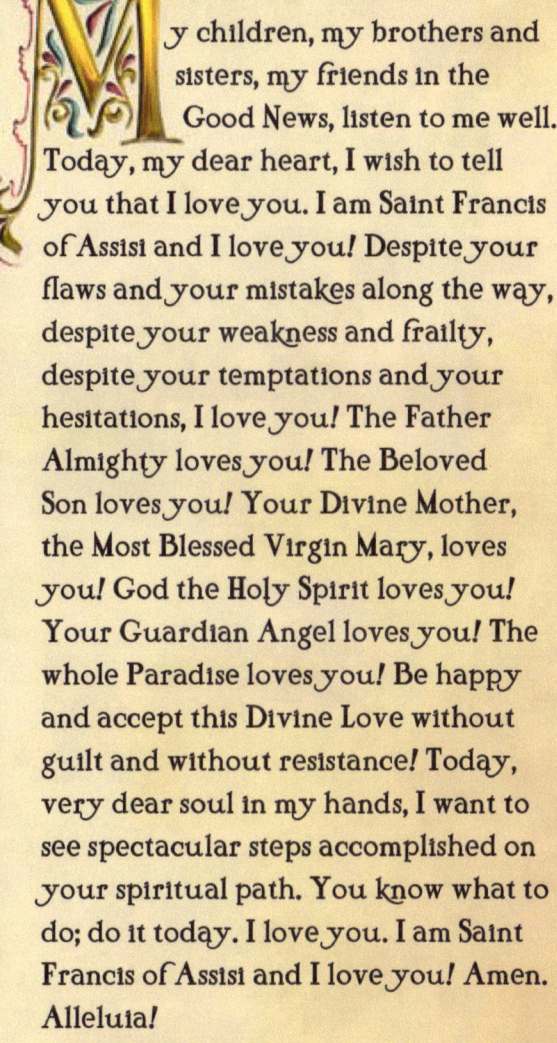

My children, my brothers and sisters, my friends in the Good News, listen to me well. Today, my dear heart, I wish to tell you that I love you. I am Saint Francis of Assisi and I love you! Despite your flaws and your mistakes along the way, despite your weakness and frailty, despite your temptations and your hesitations, I love you! The Father Almighty loves you! The Beloved Son loves you! Your Divine Mother, the Most Blessed Virgin Mary, loves you! God the Holy Spirit loves you! Your Guardian Angel loves you! The whole Paradise loves you! Be happy and accept this Divine Love without guilt and without resistance! Today, very dear soul in my hands, I want to see spectacular steps accomplished on your spiritual path. You know what to do; do it today. I love you. I am Saint Francis of Assisi and I love you! Amen. Alleluia!

Saint Francis of Assisi Speaks

My children, my brothers and sisters, my friends in the Good News, listen to me well. Today, dear heart, dear little soul in my humble hands, I am leading you into the Arms of the Holy Spirit. The Holy Spirit — God the Holy Spirit — is everywhere in the universe created by God, and His Reign, as the Reign of the Father and of the Son, will never end. He is capable of showing you the way toward the Father and toward the Son, because His Mission is one of Cosmic Mediation between your three-dimensional world and the Superior Worlds. He works always and everywhere with each one of you, although you do not notice it. He is called the Comforter Spirit, because He manifests the Divine — which is the Source of all consolation on earth — in your life. Say often today: "God the Holy Spirit, I love you; come very close to me, and show me the Father and the Son, in the Perfect Unity of the Holy Trinity, world without end, through Jesus Christ our Lord and the Immaculate Heart of Mary. Amen." Alleluia!

God the Holy Spirit,
I love you!
~ Saint Francis

Saint Francis of Assisi Speaks

My children, my brothers and sisters, my friends in the Good News, listen to me well. It is true, dear heart, that Christ Jesus is risen from the dead, and He walks among us, on earth as in Heaven. It is also true that He will return among you on earth, in the midst of a blinding and Glorious Light, in order to celebrate His Cosmic and Universal Coronation. For Jesus the Christ our Lord is the Master of the universe, and this since the beginning of the Creation and to ages of ages. Let us give thanks to God our Father for giving us His Only Son, our Lord Jesus Christ, our Savior and our God, world without end. Amen. Alleluia!

Saint Francis of Assisi Speaks

My children, my brothers and sisters, my friends in the Good News, I love you; listen to me well. Today, and for the rest of your life, remain in the Peace of Christ. The Peace of the Savior to all nations, the profound and lasting Peace sought by all, the Peace of the Kingdom of God on earth: this Peace is with you and will remain with you for Eternity. Live this Peace, experience this Peace, honor this Peace, thank this Peace; and shortly, very shortly, this Peace will cover the whole world. Amen. Alleluia!

My children, my brothers and sisters, my friends in the Good News, I love you; listen to me well. Today, I wish to see you separated from planet Earth (and of all your worries) and united with us in Paradise. Leave everything to the Father — your problems, your anxieties, your questions, your concerns — through the Wounds and Blood of Christ, and visualize Paradise around you with its inhabitants who love you all, for Paradise is really in your heart and the Divine Vibrations found therein extend very far, all around you, outside of your physical body. This is why we can share your life much more intimately than you can imagine. And most importantly, we can pray for you and perform unsuspected Miracles in the Name of Christ, our Savior and our God, and the Immaculate Heart of Mary. Stay calm and confident, abandon yourself to the Father and His Messengers, the foremost of whom is Christ Jesus, and let yourself be lulled by the Love and the Peace of the Father. Amen. Alleluia!

BLESS THE BOND
St. Francis Day/World Animal Day • October 4

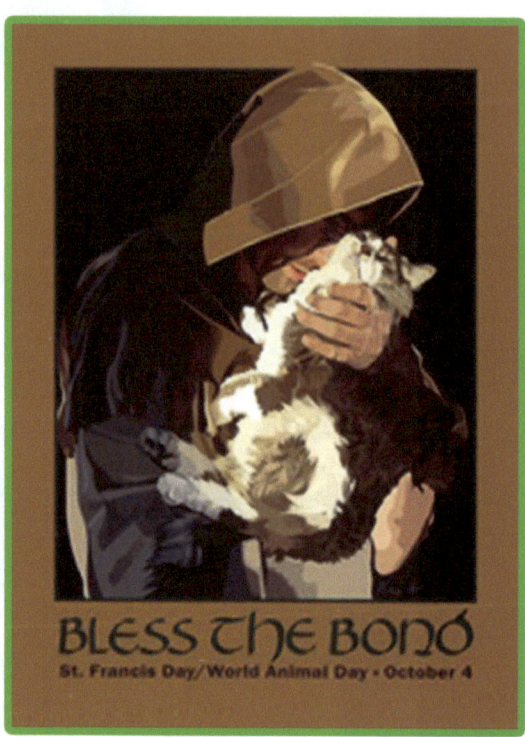

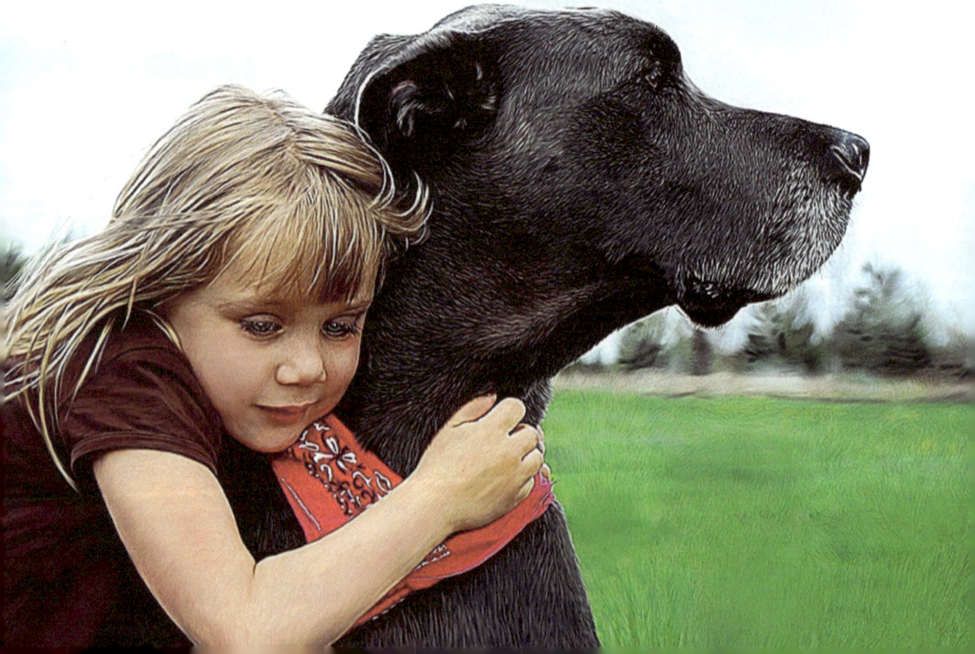

Saint Francis of Assisi Speaks

My children, my brothers and sisters, my friends in the good news, I love you; listen to me well. Today, as every day of your life, and as of now, be in a state of Grace. By this, I mean that I wish for you to be in a state of the Benediction of God, in a state of the Peace of Christ, and in a state of Clarity of the Holy Spirit — for you are. This state of Grace that is yours today, and every day for the rest of your life, will be manifested in various ways: moments of indescribable Joy, moments of spiritual Communion with the whole world, moments of sincere and profound Forgiveness, moments of unexpected Love and Charity for your fellow human beings. Today, my dear heart, you are in a state of Grace. I say unto you, I say unto you verily, and I repeat it unto you: today, you are in a state of Grace. Amen. Alleluia!

Saint Francis of Assisi Speaks

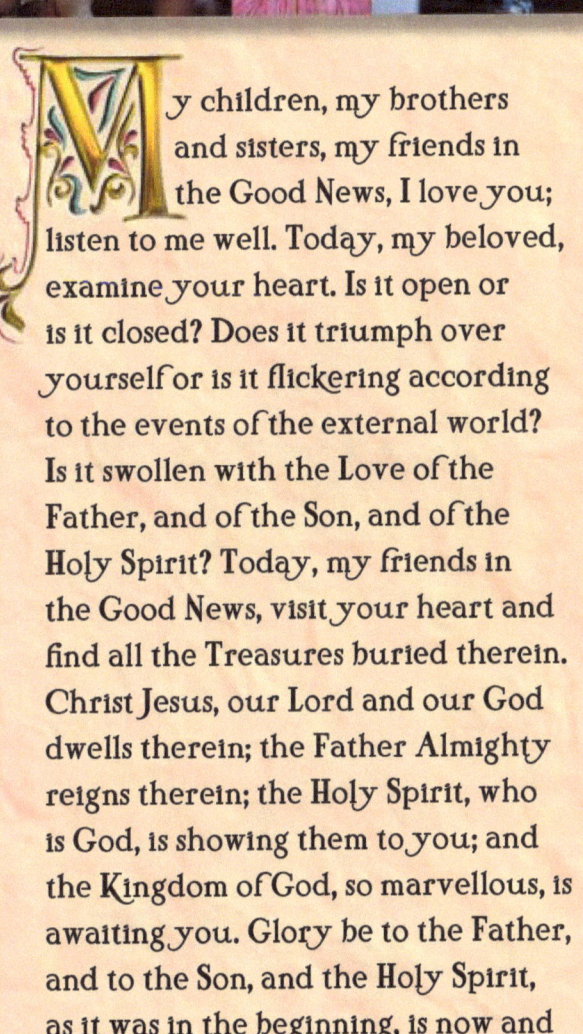

My children, my brothers and sisters, my friends in the Good News, I love you; listen to me well. Today, my beloved, examine your heart. Is it open or is it closed? Does it triumph over yourself or is it flickering according to the events of the external world? Is it swollen with the Love of the Father, and of the Son, and of the Holy Spirit? Today, my friends in the Good News, visit your heart and find all the Treasures buried therein. Christ Jesus, our Lord and our God dwells therein; the Father Almighty reigns therein; the Holy Spirit, who is God, is showing them to you; and the Kingdom of God, so marvellous, is awaiting you. Glory be to the Father, and to the Son, and the Holy Spirit, as it was in the beginning, is now and ever shall be, world without end! Amen. Alleluia!

Today, I wish to see you separated from planet Earth (and of all your worries) and

united with us in Paradise. Leave everything to the Father — your problems, your

anxieties, your questions, your concerns —
through the Wounds and Blood of Christ,

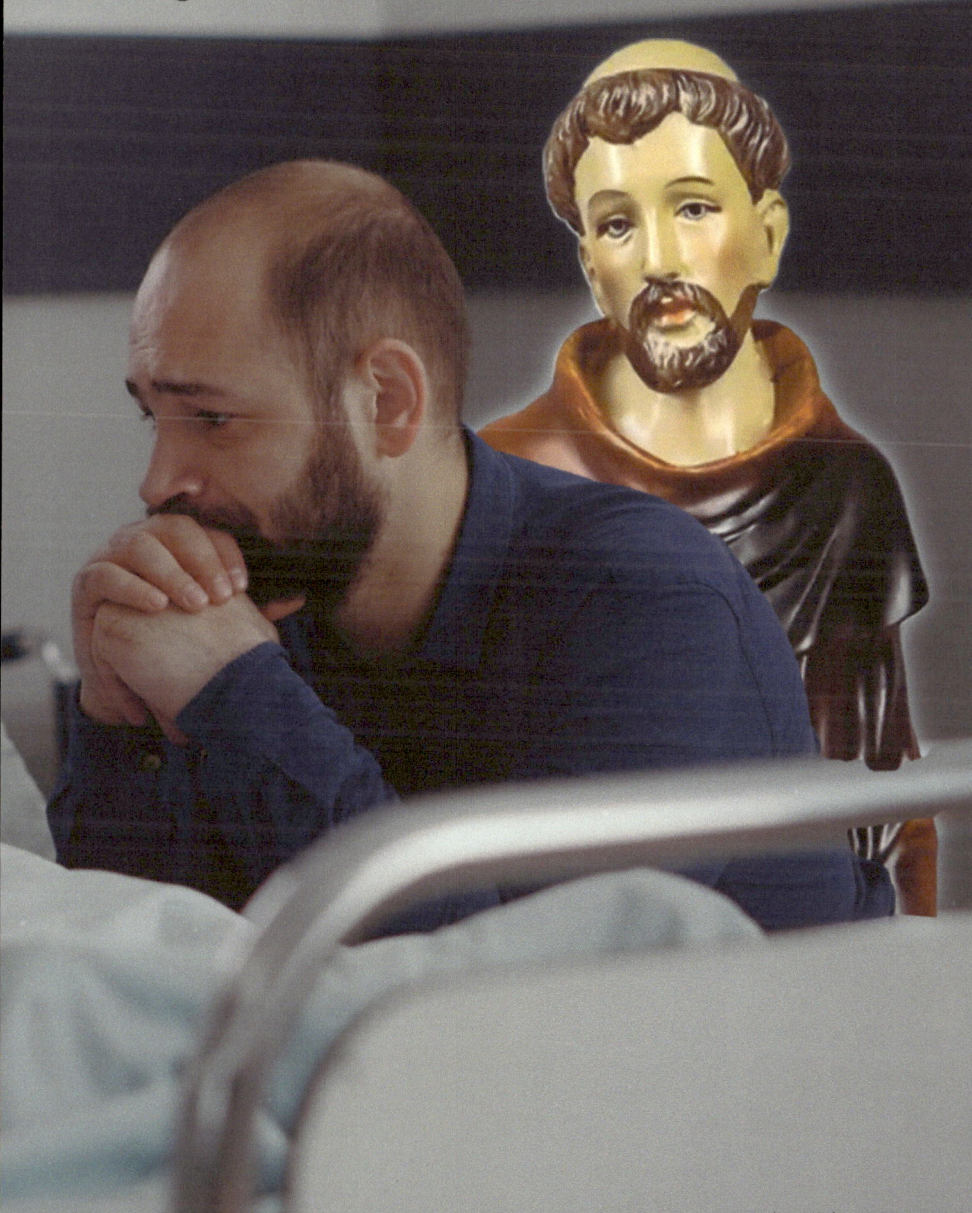

and visualize Paradise around you with its
inhabitants who love you all! ~ Francis

Saint Francis of Assisi Speaks

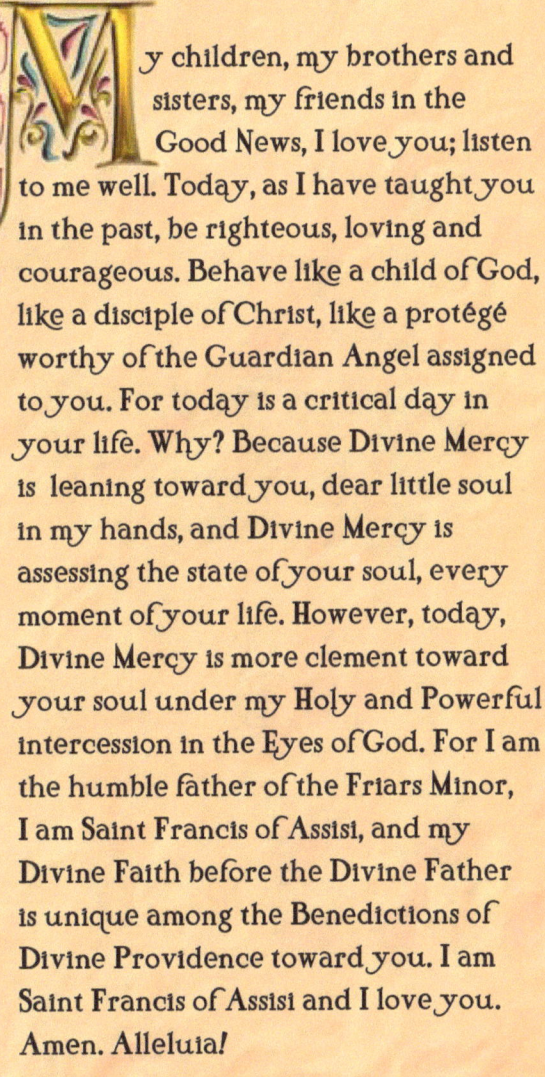

My children, my brothers and sisters, my friends in the Good News, I love you; listen to me well. Today, as I have taught you in the past, be righteous, loving and courageous. Behave like a child of God, like a disciple of Christ, like a protégé worthy of the Guardian Angel assigned to you. For today is a critical day in your life. Why? Because Divine Mercy is leaning toward you, dear little soul in my hands, and Divine Mercy is assessing the state of your soul, every moment of your life. However, today, Divine Mercy is more clement toward your soul under my Holy and Powerful intercession in the Eyes of God. For I am the humble father of the Friars Minor, I am Saint Francis of Assisi, and my Divine Faith before the Divine Father is unique among the Benedictions of Divine Providence toward you. I am Saint Francis of Assisi and I love you. Amen. Alleluia!

Saint Francis of Assisi Speaks

My children, my brothers and sisters, my friends in the Good News, I love you; listen to me well. Today, and today only, is the day chosen by God to finally set apart from you everything that is not of Christ. Everything in you that is not Light, Peace, and Love — that is to say, all your anxieties, your fears, your negativity — all of this must be simply removed from the inside of your heart and your body. In a grand gesture of self-purification, stand up, and see all the little egos attacking you (imagine small snakes, insects and monsters of all sorts) and, as if you are taking off a dirty and contaminated tunic, make the physical gesture to undress yourself and throw away as far as possible this layer of ego infestation. Your Divine Mother will be happy to step on it and eliminate it for you! Then, stand up, and walk tall and strong, as you are now healed and purified from the manipulations of the demon. Repeat this procedure often today, whenever your inner peace is disturbed, and make a decade of the rosary at that time. I love you.

Saint Francis of Assisi Speaks

My children, my friends in the Good News, my brothers and sisters, I love you so much, listen to me well. Today, my friends, pay attention to Christ who speaks with you constantly. Yes, my dear soul, Christ speaks with you much more clearly, much more often, and much more wisely than you can imagine. Christ is always there within your heart and His Powerful Presence has already been manifested in you in the past. In fact, His Majestic and Miraculous Power has brought you so far to this very moment as you are reading these Lines. Do you see? You have obeyed His commands, you have followed the given instructions, without having noted the articulation of His Words of Tenderness and Love He had addressed you. Today, my dear soul, listen religiously to your heart and take note of everything that is going on therein. For shortly, very shortly, Christ Jesus will manifest Himself even more clearly within your heart. Amen. Alleluia!

My children, my friends in the Good News, my brothers and sisters, I love you; listen to me well. Today, more than any other day of your life, be firm in your faith. The salvation of your soul is the only purpose of your life. The Mercy of God, which is given to you through these books and instructions blessed by Him, is the only wealth

Saint Francis of Assisi Speaks

that you need on earth. The Love and the Peace of Christ, which vibrate inside your heart more and more every day, is the only Presence that you need on earth. The Virgin Mary, the Most Blessed Mother of our Savior, our Lord Jesus Christ, who is your Spiritual Mother, intimate and personal, is always ready to listen to your prayers and to share your suffering. God the Holy Spirit, your Mediator of the Father and of the Son, is the only Teacher that you need on earth. Glory to God in the Highest Heaven, and Peace on earth to men of good will! Amen. Alleluia!

Saint Francis of Assisi Speaks

My children, my brothers and sisters, my friends in the Good News, I love you; listen to me well. Today, dear heart, be pure and white as snow. Dispel as soon as possible negative ideas and thoughts, meaningless or contradictory with regard to your progress on your path toward God. Do not let anything invade your peace and your inner serenity based on the Holy Trinity. If you feel weak or unsteady, say this: "O God, come to my assistance; Lord, make haste to help me!" And shortly, very shortly, the Strength, the Righteousness, and the Sovereignty of God over everything will protect you from the forces of the demon trying to weaken you on your way. Be strong! I love you. I am Saint Francis of Assisi and I love you! Amen. Alleluia!

Today, my friends, pay attention to Christ who speaks with you constantly. Yes, my dear soul, Christ speaks with you, much more clearly, much more often, and much more wisely than you can imagine.
~ Saint Francis

Saint Francis of Assisi Speaks

My children, my brothers and sisters, my friends in the Good News, I love you; listen to me well. Today, for the salvation of your soul, try to ignore the outside world surrounding you. Noise, various external energies, the contradictions of the modern world; all of this, my friends — put all of this into a ball and throw it out of your heart. For the inner life of your heart is what is important. I love you. I am Saint Francis of Assisi and I love you! Amen. Alleluia!

Today, as I have taught you in the past, be righteous, loving and courageous. Behave like a child of God, like a disciple of Christ!
~ Saint Francis

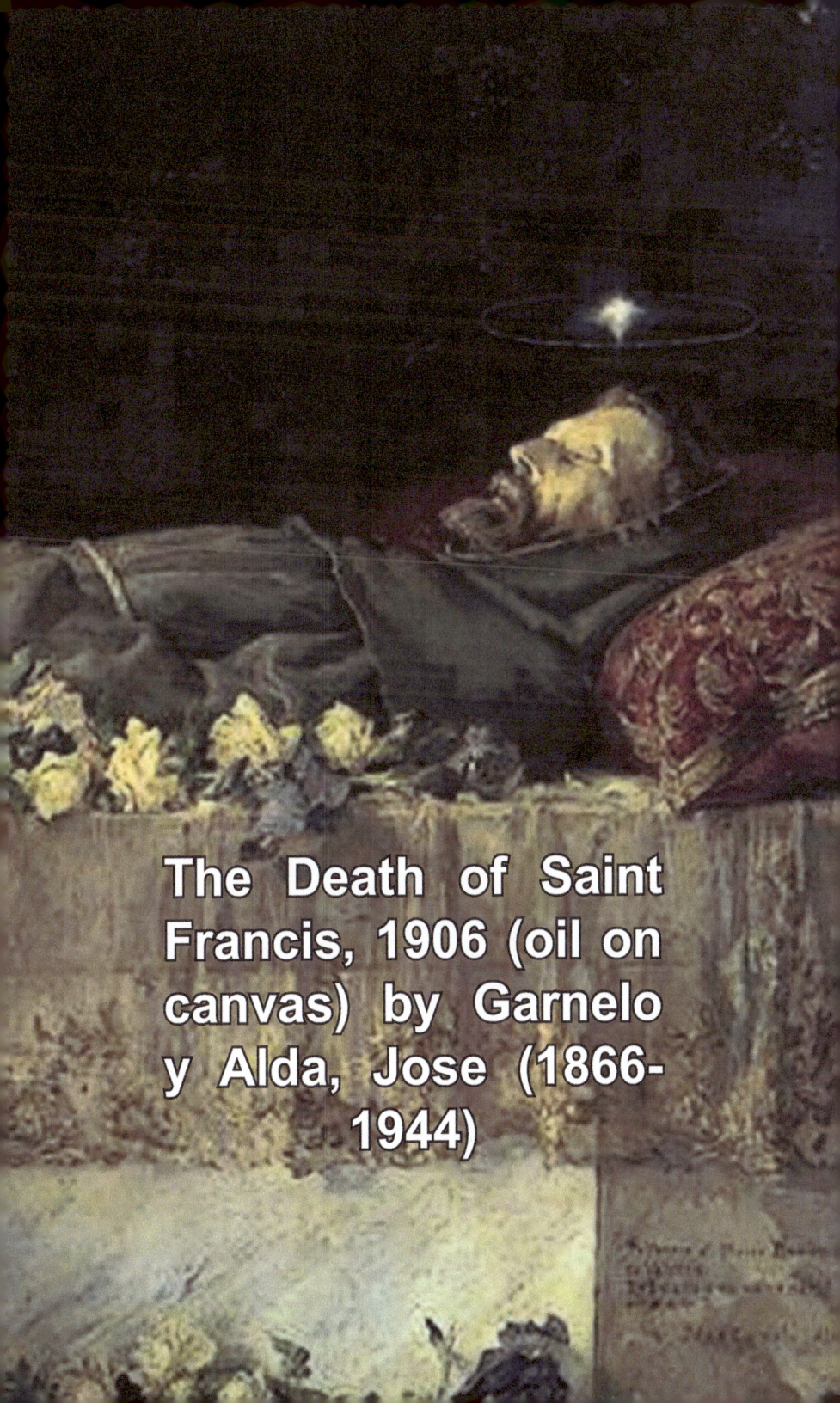

The Death of Saint Francis, 1906 (oil on canvas) by Garnelo y Alda, Jose (1866-1944)

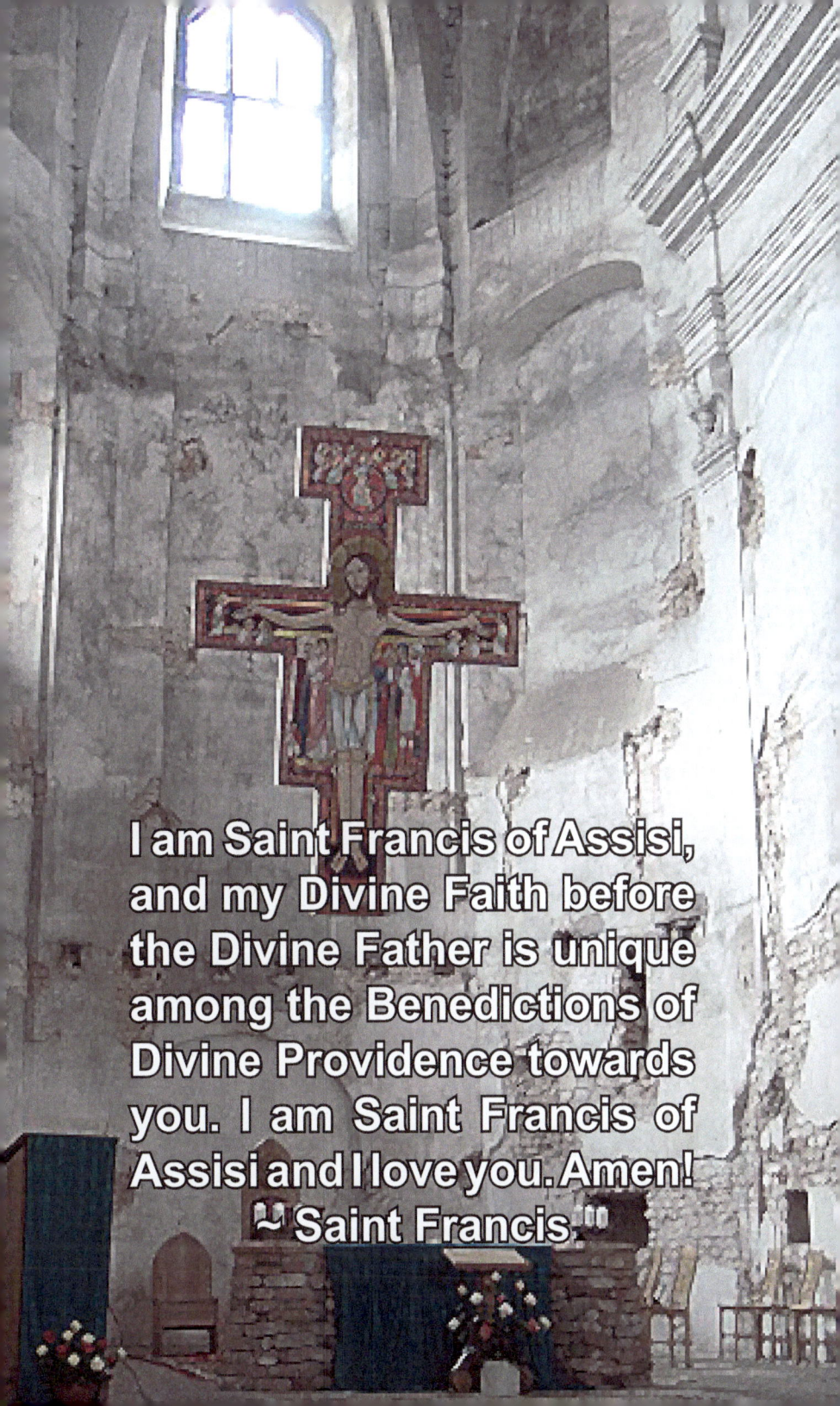

Afterword

I am always delighted to see my friend Francis visit me. He recently told me that he always accompanies Pope Francis and guides him personally.

May the great and humble father of the Friars Minor, Saint Francis of Assisi, also accompany you on your path returning back to the Father, as promised in this precious book.

Francis, I love you!

Marie-Josée

About the Author

Marie-Josée Thibault's life is in no way similar to yours. When she wakes, the saints of Heaven visit her, talk to her, teach her, and pray intensely with her. When such mystical sessions draw to a close, she greets with great respect and deep reverence the Masters of the Heavenly Court. This servant of the Lord spends the rest of the day in the company of her guardian angel, who continues her spiritual education and ceaselessly protects her from the perils of this fallen world.

Bestowed by the Heavenly Father, her gifts of clairvoyance and clairaudience allow her to remain in continuous contact with the supernatural dimension juxtaposed with ours, where the soul is born of the Spirit through Jesus and Mary. She prays that, one day soon, the entire human race will give glory to the Father, the Son, and the Holy Spirit.

Also by the Author

- Saint Padre Pio Speaks: Book 1
- Abba, Your Father, Speaks: Book I
- Abba, Your Father, Speaks: Book II
- Abba, Your Father, Speaks: Book III
- Angel Gabriel Speaks: Book 1
- Saint Beethoven Speaks: Book 1
- Dear Humanity: Book 1
- Dear Humanity: Book 2
- Saint Barnabas Speaks: Book 1
- Saint Bernadette Speaks Book 1
- Saint Therese of Lisieux Speaks: Book 1
- Saint Joan of Arc Speaks: Book 1
- Saint Martin de Porres Speaks: Book 1
- Saint John Paul II Speaks: Book 1
- Saint John Paul II Speaks: Book 2

MARIE-JOSÉE THIBAULT

SAINT

FREE DOWNLOAD

Get your free copy of :
"Saint Padre Pio Speaks: Book 1"
when you sign up to the
author's VIP mailing list!
Get started here:

www.abbamyfatheriloveyou.com

BOOK 1

www.ingramcontent.com/pod-product-compliance
Lightning Source LLC
Chambersburg PA
CBHW040455240426
43663CB00033B/19